Pirate Party

Written by Lisa Thompson
Pictures by Craig Smith and Lew Keilar

Captain Red Beard looked at the ship's calendar.

"Shiver me timbers!" he said. "Yesterday was Fingers' birthday. I forgot all about it. We must have a party for her. But it has to be a surprise."

The Captain told Fingers to stay below to mind the treasure maps.

Fingers looked unhappy.

"Dirty rotten pirates," said Fingers.

"It was Fingers' birthday yesterday and we all forgot," whispered the Captain.

"Let's have a surprise party for her today."

"Good idea," said the pirates.

Cook made the cake.

He made a giant, chocolate-cracker cake.

Fingers tried to sneak a look.

Cook had to shoo her away. "It has to be a surprise," he said.

"Dirty rotten pirates," said Fingers.

9

Bones covered the boat with streamers.

They were in Fingers' favorite colors.

Fingers loved green, red, blue, and yellow.

Fingers tried to sneak a look.

Bones had to shoo her away. "It has to be a surprise," he said.

"Dirty rotten pirates," said Fingers.

First mate Lizzie, got the games together.

"We will have *Pin the Eye Patch on the Pirate.*

Then we'll play *Race up the Rigging.*

And then of course, a treasure hunt!"

Fingers tried to sneak a look.

Lizzie had to shoo her away.
"It has to be a surprise," she said.

"Dirty rotten pirates," said Fingers.

Finally, Captain Red Beard went down below.

Fingers was sitting in the corner.
She was unhappy.

The Captain took her up to the deck.

"Surprise!" they all said together.
"Happy Birthday, Fingers."

"I made you a chocolate-cracker cake,"
said Cook.

"I did the decorations," said Bones.

"And there will be lots of games,"
said Lizzie.

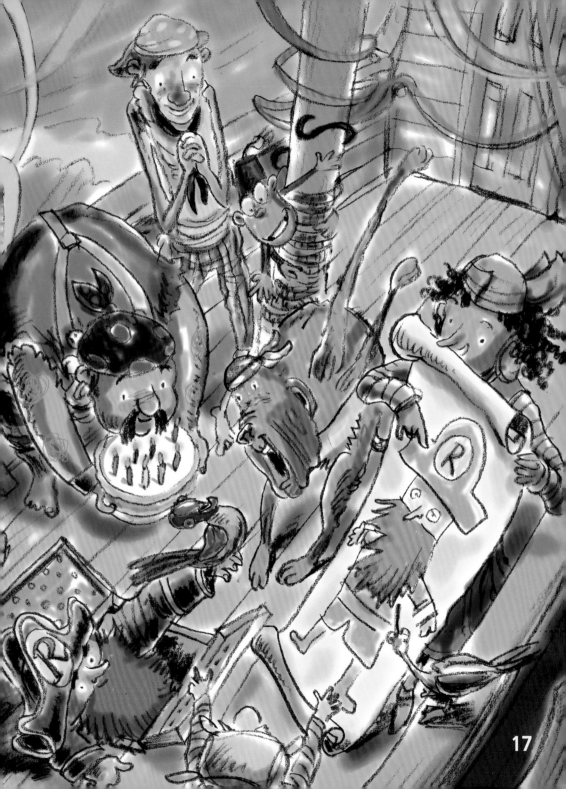

Fingers was surprised and happy.

"Nice, thoughtful, rotten pirates!"
squawked Fingers.

"Let the fun begin!" said the Captain.

Fingers gobbled up the cracker cake. Cook won the treasure hunt.

Bones looked as he pinned the eye patch on the pirate.

No one cared as they were having such a good time.

At the end of the party, Fingers gave everyone a surprise.

She bit every pirate on the finger. She nipped Bones on the ear.

"What did you do that for?" said the Captain.

"So you won't forget my birthday next year!" said Fingers.